With the author's
warmest wishes and
kindest regards,

Johnstone Patrick.

Christmas 1970.

UNDER THE MISTLETOE

UNDER THE MISTLETOE

BY

JOHNSTONE G. PATRICK

Windy Row Press

PUBLISHERS

Peterborough, New Hampshire

Printed in the United States of America

To Irene, my wife, and our children, to Vera, to
John and Mary, Jimmy and Helen, Al and Marg-
aret, Clive and Judith, and all our nephews and
nieces, for Christmas—and for keeps!

Acknowledgements and thanks are due to the editors of the following journals and periodicals in which these poems were first published and, for nostalgic reasons (since four of them are no longer with us), I list them in alphabetical order:

The British Weekly (London)
The Canadian Poetry Magazine
The Christian Century
The Christian World (London)
John O' London's Weekly (London)
The Life of Faith (London)
The New York Herald Tribune
The New York Times Magazine
Poetry of Today (London)
The Pulpit
Pulpit Digest
The Observer (Toronto)
The Villager (London)
The Watchman-Examiner

CONTENTS

I
THE SONG OF FAITH

. . . Suddenly there was with the angel a multitude of the heavenly host praising God and saying, Glory to God in the highest, and on earth peace, goodwill toward men.

—*From the Gospel According to Saint Luke.*

CAROL

1

Sing high
of Him low
in cattle-crib
and candleglow.

O glory be!
some shepherds see
time nestle in
eternity.

2

Sing low
of Him high
on scrawny Cross
against the sky.

At Bethlehem
and Calvary
the finite finds
infinity.

SHEPHERDS' DELIGHT

*You ask us why
we left our flocks?*
To marvel at
a paradox . . .

A miracle
of Death in Birth;
a Paradise
of pain in mirth;

a mystery
of Light and Love
linking earth's least
with heaven above;

a little Lamb,
in lovely zest,
at pasture on
His mother's breast;

Almighty God
some minutes old,
and small enough
for arms to hold!

THE SONG OF THE CHRISTMAS WINDS

We are the winds
that ring God's bell,
telling man of
Immanuel;

the winds that blow
and bring to earth
the Song of Faith
the angels sing;

the winds that warm
the stable-shed —
poor shelter for
so small a Thing;

the winds that weave
with Christmas care
raftered cobwebs
that heave and swing

into curtains
of softest silk
fit for the Crib
of Christ, our King.

We are the winds
that ring God's bell,
telling man of
Immanuel!

THE INFANT'S FRIENDS

There is joy and Christmas laughter
    At the coming of Christ's morn,
And the harvest of hereafter
    In the heart where He is born:

Songs of wonderment and gladness
    Fill the air,
For the Infant's friends are singing
    Everywhere!

There is beauty children borrow
    From the glow God lights once more;
Gone the sadness of each sorrow
    And the dread from every door!

Songs of wonderment and gladness
    Fill the air,
For the Infant's friends are singing
    Everywhere!

/ CHRISTMAS GREETING

The wintry winds of Christmastime,
    That sweep the eastern sky,
Have hushed their strident symphony
    To lisp a lullaby.

The big bright stars of Christmastime —
    A necklace for the night —
Braid beauty round His bracken-bed
    Like lovely candlelight.

The golden dreams of Christmastime,
    The frankincense of joy,
Are all—as myrrh—a part of Him . . .
    This bracken-bedded Boy!

The little trees of Christmastime,
    That grew where snow now drifts,
Are locked in many upper rooms
    Abloom with toys and gifts.

The cradle-song of Christmastime,
    The lyric of God's Will,
Comes carolling again to men
    Across each holy hill.

Oh, winds and stars . . . Oh, dreams and
        trees . . .
    Oh, song that angels sing . . .
Heaven and earth together greet
    The coming of their King!

A CHILD'S CAROL

I cannot sing, Lady,
  A Christmas hymn
As did the starry hosts
  Of seraphim;

Nor can I cross, Lady,
  The wold so wild
As frosted fieldsmen did
  To find your Child.

I have no frankincense,
  No myrrh, no gold,
To give your little King
  As kings of old.

Yet take my heart, Lady,
  So young and gay,
And make a home of it
  For Him on hay!

CHRISTMAS ANTIPHONY

1

Sweet is the song
that seraphs sing
to simple men
a-shepherding.

A Word-made-flesh
unfolds the plan
of man-made-God
by God-made-man.

2

Bright is the light
of every star
that fetches friends
from lands afar.

A Word-made-flesh
unfolds the plan
of man-made-God
by God-made-man.

3

Warm is the breath
of ox and ass
on Him who sleeps
in golden grass.

A Word-made-flesh
unfolds the plan
of man-made-God
by God-made-man.

4

Soft are the hands
that stroke each limb
and glad the eyes
that gaze on Him.

A Word-made-flesh
unfolds the plan
of man-made-God
by God-made-man.

5

Sharp are the sword-
shaped shades that fall
on stable-floor
and oxen-stall.

A Word-made-flesh
unfolds the plan
of man-made-God
by God-made-man.

6

Crude is the Crib
of hand-crushed hay;
cruder the Cross
on Calvary.

*That Word-made-flesh
fulfills the plan
of man-made-God
by God-made-man.*

II
THE STAR OF HOPE

. . . the star, which they saw in the east, went before them, till it came and stood over where the young child was. When they saw the star, they rejoiced with exceeding great joy . . .

— *From the Gospel According to Saint Matthew.*

THE LODESTAR

The Lodestar climbed,
Swung, poised to rest
Where Jesus lay
On Mary's breast.

God's frankincense
And gold and myrrh,
Its splendour streamed
On Him and her.

The night was calm,
The air so still,
Music haunted
The snow-hapt* hill.

The Shepherds came,
The Wise Men too,
And found the Babe
In folds of blue.

*Note: Hap, v.t. (Scottish) wrap up.

They gave their gifts,
They bowed the head;
A cock crowed thrice
Within the shed.

The Lodestar stirred
And slipped away
Over the hill . . .
To Calvary.

CHRISTMAS DAYBREAK

Sundry small clouds
were hanging white,
like swaddling clothes
to waking sight,

and as the light
of day increased
it seemed that Kings —
from storied East —

were bringing gifts;
for, lo, behold!
the firmament
was strewn with gold,

and the quick-gold
began to pour
over the earth's
snow-goose-white floor!

BABYLON AND BETHLEHEM

The Christmas Star
that brightly shone,
brought three Wise Men
to Babylon.

In Babylon —
no mean city —
they saw plenty . . .
but no pity.

The Christmas Star
still leading them,
led them at last
to Bethlehem.

In Bethlehem —
a mean city —
the three Wise Men
saw no pity;

but there — upon
the meanest bed,
within the least
inviting shed,

with company
of ox and ass,
between a lad
and lowly lass —

they found what filled
all life with joy,
the God of Love
become a Boy!

Their handkerchiefs
they then unrolled,
and Frankincense
and Myrrh and Gold —

in token of
Love's strategem —
were left behind
in Bethlehem.

THE BALLAD OF BETHLEHEM

i

A Star hung high
on Heaven's hem
brightens the black
of Bethlehem . . .

How far is it to Bethlehem?
  You Shepherds surely know,
For yesterday you saw the Light
  Across the fields of snow;
Angelic songs affrighted you,
  Yet *Faith* your footsteps led,
And you were first to worship by
  The Little Lambkin's bed.

ii

A Star hung high
on Heaven's hem
brightens the black
of Bethlehem . . .

How far is it to Bethlehem?
  You Wisemen onward ride
The many miles to Bethlehem
  Over the desert wide;

His Star shines bright above you,
    For joy His angel sings;
Ride on and *Hope* will lead you to
    The Little King of Kings.

iii

A Star hung high
on Heaven's hem
brightens the black
of Bethlehem . . .

How far is it to Bethlehem?
    You nations need to know
You missed the road to Bethlehem
    Two thousand years ago;
But those who seek may find it through
    The *Love* that flings out fears —
That old lost road to Bethlehem
    Still running down the years.

iv

A Star hung high
on Heaven's hem
brightens the black
of Bethlehem . . .

How far is it to Bethlehem?
    So many miles away

The centuries have spread a mist
    Between us and that Day;
Yet still the way goes winding, as
    A thought within a brain,
And friends fare forth to find the birth
    Of God on earth again.

v

A Star hung high
on Heaven's hem
brightens the black
of Bethlehem . . .

How far is it to Bethlehem?
    As far as folk desire
Who walk the way God wills for them
    With mind and soul afire;
For to find what all are seeking
    Men need no man-made chart —
The bracken-bed of Bethlehem
    is hidden in each heart!

HOME BY CANDLELIGHT

Aloft, in ash-bud dark,
Flickers a fitful spark,

And then there are two threes,
One more — the Pleiades.

Soon as some summer swarm,
Appears Orion's form.

Back, beyond the road's fork
Beam the lights of New York.

Above, before me now's
Heaven's many-lighted house;

A Christmas candle's lit
In every room of it.

Therein must surely be
A merry company . . .

Candles for all, God, send
To light up journey's end!

DECEMBER FOOLS' DAY

Along the avenue
   of stars
We toil toward the Moon
   and Mars.

Good God! it seems we've lost
   our mind
Since leaving Bethlehem
   behind.

STABLE - TALK

A hand is on the latch;
   Fast fly our fears.
As the door creaks open,
   Seems all our years

Have been but a schooling
   For . . . Bethlehem;
So our throbbing hearts speak
   What is in them.

Bright, and though fair, we say
   To our tall star,
The Boy will be brighter,
   Fairer by far.

No gods have we save what
   Our old hands hold —
This frankincense, this myrrh,
   This goodly gold —

And these are the love-gifts
   We'll lay, with awe,
At the feet of the God
   Asleep in straw . . .

What word was't Mary breathed
In Joseph's ear?
*Unlatch the door, my love,
Magi are here!*

WISE MEN

What do you think
We Wise Men saw
A-sleeping there
On golden straw,

And snuggled up
In swaddling clothes,
Above the thorn?—
A Christmas Rose;

An ash-tree's bud
As black as night;
The Word made flesh
In candlelight;

A Bird unsnared
Within its nest;
A Lamb unslain;
God manifest.

Gold, frankincense,
And myrrh we poured
In homage to
Our sleeping Lord.

Would we'd had gifts
Of song to sing
The praises of
That little King!

III
THE SON OF LOVE

. . . when they were come into the house, they saw the young child with Mary his mother, and fell down, and worshipped him: and when they had opened their treasures, they presented unto him gifts: gold, and frankincense, and myrrh.
— *From The Gospel According to Saint Matthew.*

. . . unto us a child is born, unto us a son is given . . .

— *From The Book of Isaiah*

THE HOUSE OF BREAD

At Bethlehem —
the House of Bread —
where royalties
again are shed

over a small
brown baby head,
pillowed upon
a bracken-bed,

the sages and
the shepherds see
the height of all
humility,

the prospect of
the Passion-tree,
an Easter of
eternity.

THE CHRISTMAS ROSE

He sleeps secure
from Herod's harm
all quick and warm
on Mary's arm.

The kings bring gifts;
one brings Him myrrh;
a sword pierces
the heart of her,

and Mary sees
the swaddling clothes,
the petals of
her Christmas Rose,

all bright and light
as gossamer,
lie neatly in
a sepulcher.

THE CHRISTMAS STORY

More thrilling than
The tall tales told
Of Rome's grandeur,
Of Greece's gold —
  So new,
  So old —

Is that which tells
To all the earth,
In pealing bells,
Of Death in Birth,
  Of pain
  In mirth;

Of kings, shepherds,
Of ox and ass,
And Child who sleeps
On golden grass;
  Of lad
  And lass;

Of angels, star,
And God come down
In flesh — from far —
To David's town;
  Of Cross,
  Of Crown!

NO WONDER IS MORE WONDERED

Wonder is not precisely knowing . . .
—Emily Dickinson (1830-1868).

Where asses' ears
and angels' wings
flicker beneath
the rafterings

a wonder wakes
more wonder than
Maid made Mother
by God made Man . . .

In a black hour,
on a low stem,
blooms the White Flower
of Bethlehem;

broken in Bread,
chaliced with Wine,
God grows human
and Man divine.

No wonder is
more wondered than
that Man made God
by God made Man!

BLEST CRIB! BLEST CROSS!

Some shepherds see
their God this Day
sleep snugly in
a nest of hay.

A customer
who deals in death
encounters Him
at Nazareth.

Athirst beside
a water-well
a woman meets
Immanuel.

A thief upon
a cross proves wise
to penetrate
Love's dear disguise.

We never know
how near He is
shrouded in small
simplicities.

Blest Crib! Blest Cross!
Blest Bench! Blest Well!
In man God comes
as man to dwell!

THE INNKEEPER

Could kick myself
I had no room
for two who came
in twilit gloom.

For in my byre —
where donkeys bray
and oxen munch
the dry, dun hay,

beyond the stall
that rodents gnaw —
their Babe was born
on bed of straw.

With tidings of
an angel-choir,
three shepherds came
to my old byre;

I laughed to hear —
it sounds so odd! —
these worshipped Him
as Lamb of God.

That night of frost,
lured by a Star,
the Three Kings rode
from lands afar;

with gifts they came
their King to greet
and bowed themselves
at the Boy's feet.

The census lined
my purse with gold;
but what is wealth
to one grown old?

Had I but known,
I'd left my bed
to sleep in that
ramshackle shed.

I'd named this inn,
for love of them,
The Little King
of Bethlehem.

THE GIFTS

God gave His Son the softness of
    a dove;
Some shepherds gave the Little Lamb
    their love;

A wise man gave the Infant King
    his myrrh,
While Mary gave her Jesus all
    of her.

Good Joseph gave his Boy a trade
    to ply;
And we? — a Tree, twisted, on which
    to die.

OX AND ASS

An ox owned sores
from blows that poured
    upon his back and side;

an ass wore welts
and weals that scored
    her dowdy, dun-hued hide.

Yet she held high
her ears, so odd,
    and he his horns, with pride;

for both shared shed
and bed with God
    one far-off Christmastide.

UNAMUNO'S CHRIST

A centenary tribute to
Don Miguel de Unamuno y Jugo
(b. Sept. 29, 1864—d. Dec. 31, 1936)

Inanimate, yet exquisite,
On Mary's knee he saw Him sit

Insensitive, sculpted in stone,
In silver frock, where priests intone

Their creed. This Christ shall know no harm;
Inside, His home is snug and warm . . .

Outside, the night is dark and cold,
Another Christ grows gray and old,

Hungry, thirsty, alive and ill,
And anguishing as on His hill.

Homeless, friendless, this Christ sublime
Is suffering till the end of time . . .

That other Christ in men must grow,
As seen by "Saint" Unamuno.

Let us defend
The right and good
From all Herodian harm and deadly
    danger!

Let us attend,
Though rough and rude,
The heart's altar of hope, and holy
    manger!

Let us extend,
In gratitude,
Life's love —at length— to a small starry
    Stranger!

LO! HERE HE LIES

1

Lo! here He lies,
the Shepherd-Lamb
angelic hosts
adore;

His sheepfold is
this stable-stall
with straw upon
the floor.

Come, horny-handed herdsmen, then,
This happy Christmas Day,
And laud the Lamb of God with lute
And bagpipes merrily!

2

Lo! here He lies,
the King of Light
angelic hosts
adore;

His palace is
this shabby shed
with starlight on
the door.

Come, magi, to the manger-throne
    This merry Christmas Morn,
Acclaim your King beneath His Star,
    The Rose above a Thorn!

3

Lo! here He lies,
the Prince of Peace
angelic hosts
    adore;

His kingdom is
this cattle-cave
with mud on door
and floor.

Come, all the world, this Christmas Night,
    Where holly-berries glow,
And kiss the God of Love —this Mite—
    Under the mistletoe!

PRAYER FOR A CHRISTMAS CHILD

Let him grow hard as hickory, as straight as
    the pine;
Grant him the gift of Thy goodness, God, this son
    of mine.

Let him be strong as the oaktree, as tall as
    the ash,
Bending, but never breaking, before winter's
    wild lash.

Give him the love of the dawn and the song of
    the bird;
Let him be honest and upright in thought, deed,
    and word.

Teach him to live and let live, with the faith of
    Thy Child,
Learning to know and befriend the shy things of
    the wild.

Make him as clean as the snow that December
    distils;
Give him the joy of the woods and the laughter
    of rills.

Then — as the hills all around him, so lovely
    to see —
Cause him to climb ever upwards and closer
    to Thee!

THREE REFUGEES

A Woman
Long ago,
In lodging
Lone and low,
  A Baby bore,

Whom herdsmen
From the hills,
Forgetting
Flocks and ills,
  Came to adore.

The magi
From afar,
Following
A fair Star,
  Brought gifts to please.

Yet no bright
Diadem
Took they from
Bethlehem —
  Three refugees.

CHRISTMAS TIDE

"He comes, comes, ever comes . . ."
—Rabindranath Tagore, (1861-1941)

Accompanied
By carollings,
God comes enwrapped
In baby things.

Beneath the cool
And candid air,
He ventures here
And everywhere.

The stable-shrine
Men seek to win
No fool need fail
To enter in,

Or miss upon
The casual street
The imprints of
The shepherds' feet.

God sends us still
His guiding Star
Where Mary and
Her Baby are,

And comes in on
This Christmas tide —
The Christ-Child and
The Crucified!

THE BLESSING

Babe of Bethlehem,
    from your starlit stable,
    straw-strewn stall,
    bless with bounty
    every table
    in earth's hall!

Man from Nazareth,
    kindle this candle's wick,
    shut the door;
    shake some shavings
    from your tunic
    on our floor!

King of Calvary,
    from Friday's healing Tree
    let fruit fall —
    in faith and hope
    and charity —
    on us all!

THE CHRISTMAS TREE

Today we touch
in stone and sod
the fingers of
a groping God,

and see in twigs
of stiff hedgerows,
or in the wood
where quiet grows

among the bare
December trees,
the Mystery
of mysteries—

the Tree of Heaven
on earth takes root;
from Jesse springs
the saving shoot.

SO SMALL A THING

You wise old ones
with costly things,
you herdsmen with
poor offerings,

you angels with
your trumpeting,
take tribute for
His hallowing

to Herod's Fool,
to Pilate's King,
to Mary's Son—
so small a Thing!

WILDING WOOD

The Crib and Cross
hold solitude,
and both are worked
from wilding wood.

His Passion-tree
of Peace yields charms,
flowering to fruit
on wooden arms.

LAMBING-TIME

Across the skies'
far frozen track
they see the sign
of Zodiac

beckoning them—
with quick-gold gleam—
to Bethlehem
of dust and dream.

And following
the big bright Ram,
they reach —at last—
the little Lamb,

dropped in bad-for-
lambing-weather,
linking God and
Man together.

IV
UNDER THE MISTLETOE

It hath been writ that anye manne
May blameless kiss what mayde he canne
Nor anyone shall say hym "no"
Beneath the holye mistletoe.

> — From *The Enchanted Oak,*
> Oliver Herford (1863-1935)

COUPLETS FOR CHRISTMAS

1

Under the mistletoe, give a kiss!
Oh, what a giving-time is this!

2

When God was only two hours old
His small brown feet grew blue with cold.

3

Men travel still—under His Star—
Hoping to find their Avatar!

4

To-night, Love, leave your door undone
For Mary, Joseph, and their Son!

5

Where Darkness makes her home in Light
Fresh Life is found on Christmas Night.

6

The Song the angels sang that Morn,
They sing when any child is born!

7

God's ways and words are weird to them
Who never went to Bethlehem.

8

That far-off song some herdsmen hear
Brings Bethlehem so very near!

9

This Christmas Day Life's Bread, Love's Wine,
Are held in Hands I hold in mine!

10

The single Star that leads to Thee,
We find, God, in Thy galaxy!

11

Love saw the sign, so Love outran
Wisdom who came by caravan!

12

The God who gathered pain from men
Comes down to gather it again.

13

All men—at Bethlehem—may find
The Christmas food for heart and mind!

14

How very close the Christ-Child is
To all life's lesser Calvaries!

15

Only in wood of Crib and Rood
Is Christmas ever understood.

16

Hold to your heart—in holy wonder—
Him who shakes the skies with thunder!

17

A Song for faith; a Star for hope;
A Son of Love for all who grope!

18

For Him who'll die on Roman rood—
A berry red as any blood!

19

To Golgotha again He'll go—
A Little Lamb as white as snow!

20

Could any tide more lovely be
That that which brings Epiphany?

21

Over the fields that Winter won
Starlight lingers, the shepherds run.

22

The great God, Love, again descends
As one more year grows old and ends!

23

What happens everywhere to-day,
First happened there, so far away!

24

How good again it is to be
In God's House of Humility!

25

Wise wolves lie down with silly sheep
And the Lamb smiles in His deep sleep.

26

Some shepherds leave a hill to roam,
And then return—enraptured—home!

27

No language is more lovely than
The new-born cry of God in Man!

28

Love all lovely, Love comes down
And Mary folds Him in her blue gown!

29

Wise are the fools who follow it—
The star some silly shepherds lit!

30

The Fire of Love that burns up fear
All men should kindle once a year!

31

The Tree that sets all life aglow,
Was once a seed beneath the snow!

32

A stable in the scheme of things
Opened the door on wonderings.

33

No man-child spoke as He who speaks
From Mamre-oak-made Crib that creaks!

34

The wintry winds God made go by
The cave in which Christ learned to cry.

35

The Word that willing handmaid heard,
Under her own heart breathed and stirred!

36

As, bough by bough, the trees grow dumb,
Carol by carol . . . Christ is come!

37

While slowly crept the caravan,
Fleet-footedly the fieldsmen ran.

38

In common ways He comes to dwell,
A King to kings! Immanuel!

39

Great ones and small ones, all remember,
A Boy once born in bleak December!

40

We keep the feast of Him on hay
In fashionable homes to-day.

41

Almighty God came down to dress
In a habit of helplessness.

42

The God who slept in innocence
Wakes up within the present tense.

43

The Darkness blossoms into Light
In the Stable on Christmas Night!

44

He who spreads each Christmas table
Was born and bedded in a stable.

45

The candle and the Christmas tree
Still keep each other company.

46

An ox looked on, within his shed,
At God asleep upon his bed.

47

Go to the Stable on Christmas Day,
And ask the Christ-Child home, to stay!

48

Without the noise of fife and drums,
The Festival of Christmas comes!

49

At Bethlehem—beyond despair—
Hail Him who wears what humans wear!

50

Under the lamp-light of this Morn,
Cry, children, cry, 'A Child is born!'

STARS

What to Wise Men
was their Star,
Poets have been—
always are!

A CHRISTMAS PLAY

A barn below
old Bethlehem
affording room
for Him and them—

Joseph, Mary,
lover and lass;
those men that came
to toss the grass;

camels, and cocks
to crow the dawn;
the ass, the ox,
a fox and fawn;

philosophers,
angels and kings;
shepherds with staffs,
scrips, stones and slings;

old Simeon,
Anna, his wife,
makers of peace
in times of strife . . .

May He who made
this multiverse
for all to bless,
for none to curse,

in this old barn—
the world's huge heart—
find room to-night
to play His part,

and Heaven will grow,
when evening falls,
once more . . . within
unpainted walls!

CHRISTMAS QUATRAINS

1

When Winter chills
the hearth of earth,
then Christmas fills
her House with mirth!

2

All eyes are blind
that never see
Christ's Cross behind
their Christmas tree!

3

Who blindly touch
Christ's wintry hem
shall leave their crutch
in Bethlehem!

4

God's speech and skin
are strange to me;
my Christmas sin
is gluttony!

5

For sheep that stray,
may shepherds pass
down every way
this Holymas!

6

When His Wind blows
where His Night snows
there always grows
His Christmas Rose!

7

God comes again
His Christmas way
to meet all men
in common clay!

THE WORD OF CHRISTMAS

Go ring your bell
and tell afresh
the fair fact of
the Word made flesh! . . .

Et verbum caro factum est!

Hard was the wood
of Roman rood;
harder to be
misunderstood!

Et verbum caro factum est!

Cold was His Crib,
but warm her breast
to lips that now
call out, 'Come . . . rest!'

Et verbum caro factum est!

Go ring your bell
and tell afresh
the fair fact of
the Word made flesh! . . .

Et verbum caro factum est!

MAN AND GOD

How good it is
for Man to see
God grow down to
humanity;

but better still
for God to see
Man grow up in
his deity!